THINGS WE LOVE

MARIANNE VICELICH

♥

"There is no friend loyal as a book."

ERNEST HEMINGWAY

National Library of Australia
Cataloguing-in-Publication entry
Author: Vicelich, Marianne
Title: Things We Love
Design and Layout: Jennifer Crooks
ISBN: 978-0-9875518-2-5 (hbk.)

Printed and Bound in China through Haha Printing
First edition published in Sydney, Australia 2013
by SEAVIEW PRESS Australia

European Distribution BOOKSPEED
16 Salamander Yards, Edinburgh EH6 7 DD

Other books by Marianne Vicelich:

BAT YOUR EYELASHES.
HOW TO BE WELL MANNERED WITH STYLE.
Published 2008

THE GLOSSY LIFE.
HOW TO BE GLAMOROUSLY ECONOMIC.
Published 2009

LOVE, LOVE ME.
Published 2011

TALK TO ME.
Published 2013

♥

To all women
- past present, and future -
who have dared to live from their heart and soul
and have had the courage to believe
that anything is possible.

It's all about you...

CONTENTS

♥

CONTENTS

♥

A SPARKLING STAR

♥

All shallow roots must be uprooted,
because they are not deep enough to sustain you.

♥

"Love sees as a child sees."

ANONYMOUS

Releasing the fun child within...

♥

Smiling is an innate human expression.
Deaf children smile. Blind children smile.
All children of all cultures smile.
Smiling is a child's first language.

Each and every child is born with an
abundance for laughter, fun, play, happiness and love.
It is part of the natural unconditioning of a child to look
for laughter, to create fun, to indulge in play,
to spread happiness and to radiate and receive love.
By contrast, fear, anger, hatred,
depression and anxiety, for instance, are not natural,
they are learned, particularly in later life
when the adult in us takes over from the child.

The newborn child wants to belong, to bond
and to be at one with his or her fellow human playmates.
Laughter connects us - both inside and out.
Through laughter, fun and play a child expresses his or her
deepest natural urges, which are to be at peace at one with all life.
None of us are ever too old to re-experience
and reclaim these natural birthrights.

♥

The one danger is that the light of our
inner child can easily become eclipsed and forgotten
if we allow ourselves to trudge tiredly,
tediously and unthinkingly into the unnatural
conditioning of adulthood.
To see life through the eyes of a child,
our own inner child,
lends a strength of peace and harmony to adulthood.
If we can see life as children do,
with their clarity and simplicity of thought, their trust,
and their innate capacity for joy and laughter,
we can find very practical solutions
to every problem we face.

Children have a fervent fascination for fun.
Give children any task or any object,
they will find fun in it.
By contrast many adults suffer from over-seriousness,
depression and other forms of spiritual malnourishment.
They misplay, forget or neglect to tend their natural love of fun.
If you are wise you will never overlook the importance
of fun in your life.
To allow a spirit of fun to carry you along in life
is the mark of creative genius.
To invest a sense of fun into everything you
do fires your creative imagination.

♥

Adult geniuses such as
Albert Einstein or Thomas Edison
invested huge amounts of fun into their work.
It was a spirit of fun and adventure
that fuelled their enthusiasm.
What is the outstanding characteristic of a small child?
It is enthusiasm.
They think the world is exciting,
everything fascinates them ...

The fun child within us is an entrepreneur,
an explorer and an adventurer.
Our instinctive capacity for fun feeds our curiosity,
our creative conjecture and contemplation.

My favourite thing is to go where I have never been.
Each and everyday is a new life,
a fresh beginning and an unexplored
opportunity for the fun child in us
- by contrast the adult in us
believes he or she has seen it all before.
Each and every day it is good to
let your inner child wander
through a world that is truly new.

♥

♥

*"Being silly is not silly;
being silly is a first step to being free."*

R.HOLDEN

The word silly is derived from two old European words;
seely and saelig, both of which mean 'blessed', 'happy' and 'joyful'.

Silliness offers a natural,
easy source of happiness and merriment to children.
To be silly also serves some very serious function in early life.
A child needs silliness for healthy,
creative mental and emotional growth;
so too do adults.

One of the most important functions of silliness
is that the act of being silly helps to keep the mind young,
fresh, alive and relatively unconditioned.
The less silly a person is
the more conditioned he or she becomes.
Silliness allows the mind to breathe easy
and to be free from the cobwebs and constraints of conformity,
seriousness and dull,
adult conditioning and limitation.

Silliness often inspires creativity, original thought,
invention and innovation. Copernicus, the Polish astronomer,
was at first considered silly for stating that the sun,
not the earth, was the centre of the solar system
and Alexander Graham Bell's idea
for a telephone sounded initially very silly.

The newness of life game...

♥

The Indian poet Rabindranath Tagore
said each day is a new day
that has never happened before.

Young children live in the moment;
their senses of sight, hearing,
touch, taste and smell are all finely attuned
to the new, the novel and the now.

Each and every day we are born anew,
if we allow ourselves to be.
Each day, by way of celebrating you are alive,
challenge yourself,
as a child would to experience something new.
Make today a new beginning.

Life as a learning game...

♥

Learning is a life-long experience.
All the world is a school, all the world is a playground.

It was Henry Ford who wrote,
'Anyone who stops learning is old,
whether at 20 or 80.
Anyone who keeps learning stays young.
The greatest thing in life is to keep your mind young.'

There is always something new to learn.
Robert Fulghum's book,
All I Need To Know I learned In Kindergarten states:

All I really need to know about how to live
and what to do and how to be I learned in kindergarten.
Wisdom was not at the top of the list,
but these are the things I learned.

· Share everything.

· Play fair.

· Don't hit people.

· Put things back where you found them.

· Clean up your own mess.

· Don't take things that are not yours.

· Say you are sorry when you hurt someone.

· Wash your hands before you eat.

· Flush.

· Warm cookies and cold milk are good for you.

· Live a balanced life - learn some and think some
and draw and paint and sing and dance
and work every day some.

· Take a nap every afternoon.

· When you go out into the world,
watch out for traffic,
hold hands, and stick together.

· Be aware of wonder.

· Goldfish and hamsters
and white mice they all die.
So do we.

· And then remember the first word you learned
- the biggest word of all - look.

The playtime game

♥

Know the value of playtime.
Each and every day of your life
set aside a little time for play.
Allow the spirit of play to be present in all that you do.
One of the saddest sights you will see in life
is an adult who has forgotten how to play.
So much of what we treasure, value and aspire to
can be achieved through play,
such as laughter, friendship, fun, creativity,
relaxation, freedom from worry,
union, joy and shared experience.

The wonder games

♥

A newborn child exudes energy, vitality and spirit.
By contrast, the average adult lopes along in life
mostly in neutral gear. He or she is taking it mostly for granted
and has apparently seen it all before.
To keep happy, you must keep cultivating wonder.

Dr William Fry, MD, dedicated over 30 years
to researching the potential therapeutic properties
of humour and laughter.

Dr Fry describes laughter as a total body experience
in which all the major systems of the body such as the muscles,
nerves, heart, brain and digestion participate fully.
The overall physical effect of laughter takes place,
on the whole, in two steps:

STEP 1

Healthy stimulation.

STEP 2

Deep relaxation.

First, with the advent of mirth,
your body is manipulated and exercised;
second the afterglow of mirth, your body becomes relaxed
and soothed. Such is the profound effect that ventilates
the lungs and leaves muscles, nerves and heart warm and relaxed.
Laughter, like physical exercise, speeds up heart rate,
steps up blood-pressure, quickens the breathing,
expands circulation and
enhances oxygen intake and expenditure.

Dr Fry's research demonstrates that laughter exercises
not only the upper torso, lungs and heart
but also certain muscle groups in the shoulders,
arms, abdomen, diaphragm and legs.
He goes so far as to say that 100 to 200 laughs a day
is the equivalent to about 10 minutes of jogging.

The famous nineteenth-century philosopher
Herbert Spencer was one of the first serious scientists
who alluded to the massaging effect of laughter,
in his 1860 work *The Physiology of Laughter*.
He believed that laughter serves as a wonderful safety-valve
for coping with an 'overflow of nerve force'
and for discharging 'disagreeable muscular motion'.
He was convinced that laughter is an essential
mechanism for restoring physical comfort,
biological harmony and internal order.

While laughter cannot cure pain,
it is evident that laughter can help to facilitate
genuine pain release.
The ability of laughter to relax muscle tension
and to soothe sympathetic nervous system stress
can certainly help to promote pain control.
Deeper breathing and an enhanced circulation,
as inspired by laughter, can also help minimise pain.
Medical research has also found that laughter can
activate a release of two neuropeptide chemicals
- endorphins and enkephalins.
Both are commonly described as
the body's natural pain suppressing agents.
The action of laughter also releases catecholamines,
which together with adrenalin and noradrenalin,
are thought to enhance blood flow,
reduce inflammation, speed the healing process
and heighten the overall arousal of the body.

Happiness is an attitude

♥

The most wasted day is that
in which we have not laughed.
Happiness happens inside-out, not outside-in.
There is no magical formula
that states that X per cent of status or wealth
will guarantee happiness.
To be happy, you must think yourself happy.
Happiness is the product of mind,
of attitude and of thought.
Happiness comes from you, not to you.

Happiness is a perception

♥

If you look for happiness, happiness will find you.
Many people make themselves unhappy
in life because they look for all the things in life
they either haven't got or cannot have,
they rarely take the time to look at,
acknowledge and appreciate all that they have got.

Happiness is a talent

♥

Happiness is not a gift given to the chosen few.
Happiness is a talent and a skill.
Happiness is like a muscle -
it needs to be flexed and exercised.
Happiness happens if you let it
and is only ever a thought or feeling anyway.

Happiness is a way of travelling

♥

Happiness is not so much a final destination
as a way of journeying through life.
There is no need to save up all your happiness
for an event or goal somewhere into the distant future,
look for happiness today, along the way, as you go.
Benjamin Franklin said,
"Human felicity is produced not so much
by great pieces of good fortune that seldom happen
as by little advantages that occur every day."

Happiness is a little

♥

If you cannot be happy with a little,
it is very likely that you will be happy with a lot.
Practice happiness first on a small scale
and work your way up from there.
A great obstacle to happiness is to anticipate
too great a happiness.
Great expectations make for small compensations.

Happiness is loyalty

♥

To be happy it helps to be loyal
- to your family, to your friends, to your values
and, above all, to yourself.
Be true to your own vision
and the people who genuinely love you
will be thrilled for you.
Trying to find happiness
by following other people's ideas of it rarely works.
Be true to your own vision.

Happiness is shared

♥

"All whom joy would win, must share it
- happiness was born a twin", wrote Lord Byron.
One of the most important lessons of life
is the lesson that states, quite simply,
that what you give is what you get.
If personal happiness is one of your ultimate goals in life,
then giving a portion of this happiness
back to others has to be very high on your list
if you are to succeed.
Happiness is a gift for others

There is an insect
that lives in the heart of the Amazon
that has a lifespan of 59 minutes.
After I first heard about this insect
I became for a short time, obsessed with this thought:
If I were to live for just one hour,
what would I do to make it a happy one?
The joy of this game is that it makes you
stop putting happiness on hold.
You can experience it now, not after, if, when or then.

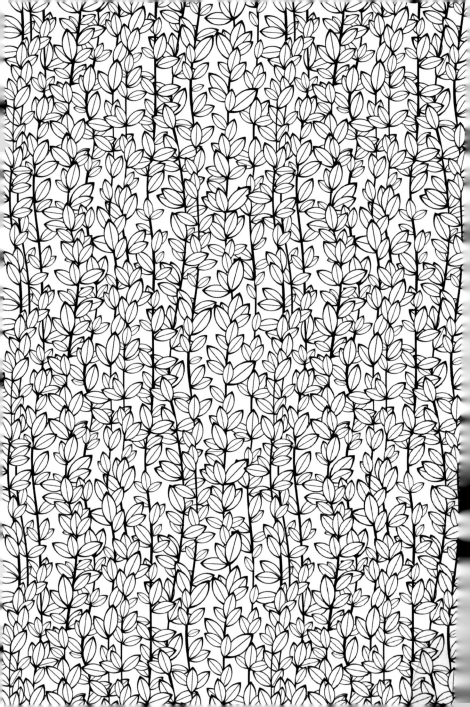

CHAPTER 2

SET YOURSELF FREE

♥

"The key to happiness
is the decision to be happy."

A RETURN TO LOVE BY MARIANNE WILLIAMSON

♥

The journey we undertake together
is the exchange of dark for light,
of ignorance for understanding.

Nothing you understand is fearful.
It is only in darkness and in ignorance
that you perceive the frightening,
and shrink away from it to further darkness.

And yet it is only the hidden
that can terrify, not for what it is,
but for its hiddenness.

♥

When sad, sing

♥

A Japanese study has found we may actually derive positive and even romantic emotions from listening to sad songs.

Scientists at the Tokyo University of the Arts
and the RIKEN Brain Science Institute in Japan asked
44 volunteers to listen to sad songs and rate their perception of
the song and their emotional state after hearing it.

Sad music was perceived to be more tragic,
whereas the actual experiences of the participants
listening to the sad music induced them to feel more romantic,
more blithe, and less tragic emotions
than they actually perceived with respect to the same music.

Ai Kawakami, who ran the study, said
"Emotion experienced by music has no direct danger or
harm unlike the emotion experienced in everyday life.
Therefore, we can even enjoy unpleasant emotion such as sadness.
If we suffer from unpleasant emotion evoked through daily life,
sad music might be helpful to alleviate negative emotion."

Balancing yourself

♥

Balance is one of the key elements for your wellbeing.
Try to imagine an old-fashioned weight scale
- to balance the scales you need to put equal parts
of your life on either side. Too much on one side will topple
the scale, but when you place just the right amounts on either side,
you find a force that's balanced and powerful.

Everyone needs a little time to nourish their souls
and get back in touch with who they are and what they want.
Sometimes the routine you have
and the constant commitments you make
throw you off the track of where you want to go.
By choosing how you are going to be no matter
what life throws at you, enables you to live the life you choose to.
It is also important to take time out to relax,
appreciate and reflect.

When you are in a relaxed state of mind
you are able to see things clearer, find a solution
to that problem you were mulling over
and even just reaffirm where you are and where you want to be.
When you are calm, relaxed and peaceful,
you get back in touch with who you are.

Tips for getting balance back in to your life

♥

Pamper yourself and get a massage or take a bath.
Spend time with your pets.
Spend time in nature, at parks, beaches or just in the garden.
Take your shoes off and connect with
Mother Nature.

Make sure you get enough sleep during the night.
Otherwise take a short nap during the day.
Meditate or sit quietly,
just focusing on your breath for 20 minutes.

Do some exercise.
This is a great way to release endorphins,
feel-good chemicals in the body that reduces stress.
Be productive.
Make a list of things you have to do for the day
and organise the list by importance.
In this way you can take care of things
before they become a problem.

Nature heals us

♥

We are part of nature.
We are affected by the change in the seasons
and the cycles of the moon. As indigenous people put it,
the earth has a heartbeat and we are one with
the heartbeat from the earth.

When we perceive ourselves as separate,
we are cut off from living in the harmony and flow of nature.
We separate ourselves from the nurturing
we receive from the elements -
earth, air, water, and fire in the form of sun.

When we are in a harmonious state
where we experience in our bodies the connection with nature,
the web of life, and our spiritual light,
we too are in a state of coherence,
all our cells communicating with one another in concert
in a beautiful symphony.
It is when we experience ourselves as separate
and we move into triggered reactive states
or states of stress that our cellular communication
breaks down and makes us ill.

Living in the moment

♥

When you are feeling balanced
you will find you are also centred on the present moment.
This is something I believe is invaluable
if you want to be more relaxed and in control of your life.
Living in the moment is letting go of all that stress
and worry that you have accumulated
and not projecting those negative emotions
on your future actions. It's more about working actively
towards your goals and dreams
without constantly stressing about how you are
going to achieve them or replaying past mistakes in your head.
In this way, we don't judge the moment we are in,
but accept it for what it is.
Every moment that we enter is like a blank canvas,
it's our emotions and thoughts that colour what we see.
When you are in the present moment it's easier to accept
the reality of the situation that you are in.
When you embrace the way things are in the moment,
you start the process of change,
and you allow new possibilities to emerge.

Use life as a mirror of your inner belief system

♥

Shakti Gawain, author of Living In The Light,
popularised the concept that the world is our mirror,
we get back a response from others that mirrors our thoughts.

If you feel unlovable,
you will fend off the admiration of others.
If you fear success at work, you will find ways to validate
that belief through self-sabotaging behaviour.
If you feel victimised by life events,
you will act out this role in relationships,
by rejecting responsibility.

There is an Indian belief
that everyone is a house of four rooms,
a physical, a mental, an emotional, and a spiritual room.
Most of us tend to live in one room most of the time,
but unless we go into every room every day,
even if only to keep it aired, we are not complete.

If you find that your life has a singular focus,
take a four-sided approach to creating satisfaction.
Spend some time each day in each of these four 'rooms',
mental, emotional, spiritual and physical.

CHAPTER 3

BRINGING SERENITY BACK

♥

"My happiness is an inside job."

LOUISE L. HAY

Jealousy and envy...

♥

Jealousy can be a powerful emotion
if it is given the opportunity to spiral out of control.
You won't be able to slay this monster
with a traditional sword and shield
and you definitely can't close your eyes and hope it goes away.
At some point everyone has experienced jealousy and envy,
and it doesn't feel good.

I believe jealousy is all about negative power and attention.
The core of jealousy is inadequacy.
Jealousy is present when our sense of self is put at risk.
When we feel this emotion it is akin to having an
identity crisis and it is a calling within us to better ourselves.
If you are truly comfortable in your own skin
and confident in your own abilities
you can transform jealousy into acceptance.

Jealousy is not the same as healthy competition.
When it comes to sport or business success, healthy competition
can motivate and push you to achieve your goals. It is important to
remind ourselves that we are all perfect exactly the way we are.
We all have strengths and weaknesses
and we also have the resources we need to improve ourselves.
We have the responsibility to ourselves to discover
what makes us distinctive and to further develop our talents.
It doesn't help to wait for the approval of others to feel good.
Work on accepting yourself as you are
and become the best version of you that you can be.

We often compare ourselves to others, imagining that
someone else has a better life, or a happier marriage or
a more satisfying career than we do.
The truth is that is pure projection.
The reason we project is that we don't always have
an accurate reflection of ourselves. We cannot always see what
we do have in our life and who we really are. So we look outside
ourselves and use others as a mirror, a basis for judgments about
our lives. Material wealth does not create happiness.
On the contrary, some of the wealthiest people I have worked with
are also the unhappiest people I know. I have seen people
who live in poverty who have a presence that lights up any room
they are in. The quality of laughter in their eyes is the envy of those
whose eyes are filled with emptiness and suffering.

Some sense of competition can serve us well.
It is often through feeling competitive
that we strive to be the best we can,
so this can inspire us to keep working and growing.
But you know what deep jealousy and envy can feel like,
jealousy might be a lover flirting,
envy is desiring what someone has.
And they hurt both your body and your psyche.
It hurts the people you feel jealous and envious of, too,
as you rob their energy. When we move into strong feelings
of jealousy and envy, we are coming from a place of lack,
from the experience that our cup is half empty.
And yet creation comes from a place of abundance.
You cannot create from a place of lack.

So what do you do when you move into this frame of mind,
negatively comparing yourself to others?
First you must remember that,
like diamonds, we all manifest different facets of beauty
and brilliance in the world.

I have never seen a group of people
comparing the beauty of stars in the night sky.
Nor have I heard people comparing the beauty of flowers.
We might feel drawn to one flower over another,
but we honour all flowers for the beauty they possess.
We must treat one another - and ourselves - the same way.

We all have a destiny, but at the same time
we also have the opportunity to make choices.
We can create happy lives with what we are given.
Or we can choose to be bitter over what life gives us.
It is important for us to see that by choices we make,
we can grow, learn, and evolve.

When people near the end of their life
share their experience of reflecting on their lives,
they say it is the small acts of kindness
remembered that bring them comfort and peace.

The more you can acknowledge
your own personal beauty and brilliance,
the less you will compare what you have
or what you perceive that you don't have with others.
The more you can appreciate who you have become
through your life experiences,
the more wealth you will feel inside.
The more richness you feel in acknowledging
your own strengths and beauty,
the less you will look outside of yourself
and compare yourself with others.

This requires taking some time each day
to go within and reflect on what you do have
and what you have done in the world.
You can do this in the morning before you start your day.
Or you can make it a practice before you go to sleep each night.

In time you will create a peace inside that you
wouldn't trade with another human being on the planet.
And from this place of abundance
you will begin to experience the unlimited possibilities
you have to create in your life.

Focusing.
Turning Your
Energy To A
Positive Frequency

♥

When I decide to be happy
I attract great things in my life.
I have a beautiful life filled with happiness
and love and I am rewarded with
all the joy life can offer.
I naturally attract great things in my life.

Everything I have has been created by me ...

♥

"Humour is a whisper from
the soul, imploring mind
and body to relax, let go and
be at peace again."

♥

Perception has a focus.
It is this that gives consistency to what you see.
Change but this focus,
and what you behold will change accordingly.

Focused energy

♥

Remember like attracts like.
Therefore the energy that's vibrating inside you
will bring similar energy to you.
When you are vibrating on a super-cool frequency,
then what comes your way will be equally as cool.
But tuning your energy to your frequency of choice requires focus.
Without proper focus you open yourself up to the random energy
of the Universe. We are all magnets capable of attracting
at all times. But your negative thoughts and feelings
represent a brick wall that lies between you
and all you are capable of attracting. Your main block is that you
don't know the power you have over your energy.
The ego always speaks first. Its voice is always the loudest,
and it is always wrong. The ego screams that you have to
control everyone and everything in order to get what you want.
The ego tells you to fear people, not to expect anything good
out of life, and to worry about all outcomes.
Identifying with this fear talk has deprived you of working
with your inner source of power.

The future and the past are preoccupations of the ego.
The only time that matters is right now. Fear of the future blocks
you from enjoying the moment and co-creating with the Universe.

Unfocused energy

♥

Without clear focus, you might be stopping yourself
from achieving all the positivity
the Universe has in store for you.
Focused energy can act as a road map.
Surrender to the energy and you will feel guided,
even when you arrive at what at first seems like a detour.
When your energy is tuned in to a positive vibration,
you can have faith that you are always
being guided either toward your desires or to a detour that will
bring you something better. Stop blocking yourself from
golden opportunities and start focusing.
Why try to navigate through life without a road map or a GPS?
Tap into your inner guide and let the Universe help
with your sense of direction. If you are controlling
or manipulating outcomes of your life's circumstances,
that's a sure sign that you are not focusing on your inner energy.

In order to focus your energy in a positive way,
you must feel positive.

♥

Try this focusing meditation for thirty days and repeat daily ...

Close your eyes and take a deep breath,
in through your nose and out through your mouth.

Hold a vision in your mind of a person,
place or situation that makes you happy.

Sit for a moment and let your mind create story angles
and images that connect with this vision.

As you breathe in,
connect with the feelings of happiness that these visions ignite.

As you exhale, release these happy thoughts into the Universe.

Continue to breathe in joyful feelings and identify
where they are held in your body.

Breathe directly into that area of your body, accessing a
closer connection to your feelings of joy.

Feel energy inside you vibrate as you exhale it out into the Universe.
Practice enhancing the energy with each inhale.

Share this energy with every exhale.

The glass is always half full...

♥

The benefit of being positive
is something that we hear continuously.
Research by Dr Masaru Emoto, conducted on water crystals
demonstrates this. Dr Emoto did a study on how energy,
thoughts, words and even music affected water.
He started by freezing a tiny portion of water
that had been taken from various parts of the world
and photographed their molecular structures.
He made some amazing discoveries
on how saying words of love and gratitude around water,
even thinking it, could change its structure
into something like the form of a beautiful snowflake
and how saying negative words
could make the water structure look eroded and splotchy.
Taping words of 'hope', 'peace', 'thank you'
and 'I love you', to glasses of water
had a profound effect almost immediately,
as well as the words 'hate', 'ugly', 'fat'.

The result was that we always observed
beautiful crystals after giving good words,
playing good music, and showing,
playing, or offering pure prayer to water.
The study suggested that the combination
of non-resonating vibration can result
in destructive energy,
and nothing can be created out of it.
When some vibration and the other
resonate each other,
it always creates beautiful design.
Thus, most of the Earth
is covered with beautiful nature.

Scientists have long proven
that everything is made out of energy.
If we break things down we can see how matter is
made out of atoms, and if you break that down further
you will see that atoms are just vibrating energy.
It is the same with water and also with our bodies.
The study showed that about 70 per cent
of the average person is made up of water.
Our thoughts and words
have a profound effect on our bodies too.

The Forest and the Trees...

♥

Mindfulness means both awareness of ourselves
in the present moment
and an appreciation of our connection to the rest of life,
giving rise to a need for thoughtful,
careful attention.

Attached to the heart....

♥

Many cultures locate the mind at the heart centre.
When we open our minds to a real sense of interconnectedness,
we find our hearts open as well.

Treat life as a precious gift...

♥

In the end, it is a matter of choice.
How do you want to spend your life?
It's your time to spend as you wish.

I believe we are far better off if we treat life
as the precious gift that it really is.
But it's a gift we ultimately have to relinquish.
Grasping it like a miser while we are alive
will not help us develop real appreciation for it.
In order to know how to spend it wisely
we need to develop mindfulness.

Valuing mindfullness...

♥

Attention has great power to overcome tensions,
habits, and the negative emotions that give rise to suffering.

Our joy and appreciation of our lives
are robbed by our negative qualities,
which lead us to suffering again and again.
To free ourselves from the grip of these qualities,
so that we can benefit ourselves and others,
we need to develop attention.

Mindfulness helps steady, stabilise, and strengthen
the power of our attention and increases our 'centre of gravity'
so we become less easily swayed by distraction.

Seeking out stillness

♥

Try to begin and end each day with a moment of stillness.

If you can take a moment to settle yourself
before the rush of the day begins, it can act like an anchor,
a reminder that there is silence even amid the flurry.

Before extinguishing the lights at the end of the day,
look again for the stillness that was always there,
even as you had to dash through the events of the day.

During the day,
there are often opportunities to touch this silence,
if only for a moment. Look for them, if you can,
and take the moment for yourself.
It requires no ostentation or special pose,
just an acknowledgment that the silence is there.
It is always there.

Atisha, the great Buddhist teacher
from twelfth-century India, said,
"When in company, check your speech.
When alone, check your mind."

Mindfulness is the awareness of actions, words, and thoughts.
All three realms hold the potential for positive and negative activity.
Lacking awareness, we are prone to thoughtless action.
We have all experienced the damage wrought by careless words
and actions at one or another. Because they are the source of negative
words and actions, mindless thoughts can be equally damaging.

Habitual tensions in the body are a consequence
of a lack of awareness. The habitual thinking that many of us
are subject to is also the result of a lack of awareness.
When we turn our attention to our thoughts, we begin to see how
capricious and unruly they appear. Instead of being guided
by intention, most of the time our thoughts are pushed and pulled
by delusion. Traditional teachings describe six principle delusions
- ignorance, attachment, anger, pride, wrong views and doubt.

Doubt hinders our progress by compelling us to
tread the same ground over and over. Rather than questioning
a point, examining it, deciding upon its validity,
and then applying it to practice, we circle around and around
so that we can no longer rely on our intelligence and experience.
If we do not trust our intelligence and our own experience,
we can never hope to find our way out of the forest of delusion.

A shift happens when you let go. Holding onto past situations
inhibits your growth. Choose to let go of past hurts.
Each day is a new beginning and an opportunity to grow.

Love attachement

♥

We all wish for love, to feel love and to express it.
Even the most hardened heart is closed only because it lacks love.
But attachment often masquerades as love.
It is only when it is put to the test that we see its true colours.

We could benefit by a lesson from the bees.
They make small but repeated efforts,
day in and day out over the course of summer.
Drop by drop, they bring in the nectar
of a season's worth of flowers and refine it to its essence.
By working steadily, they gain a hive full of honey by Autumn.
Patient, steady effort, a little each day, will lead to results.

Appreciation

♥

Each day when you awake,
you can appreciate the fact that you are alive, that you have one
more day to work towards your benefit and that of others.
You can remind yourself that life is rare and precious and you would
like to make the best use of it while you have the opportunity.

♥

You can begin your day by setting your motivation.
How do you want to live your life?
What do you want to accomplish?
These are your motivations.
You may have objectives in the world, to achieve success.
You can also have inner goals,
to help yourself and others become more compassionate.

♥

We drift all the time, startled to find our thoughts
have carried us a million miles away.
As you go through the day, you can use the day's activities as a
reminder to bring your attention back to the moment.
Any simple act will do.
Each time you sit down or stand up, you can set 'alarm clocks'
in your mind to bring you back to your attention.

♥

Try to recognise our additions to our negative emotions.
Each of these delusions - anger, attachment, pride,
jealousy, ignorance, has an antidote.
Anger is subdued by patience,
attachment by understanding impermanence.
Pride is countered by recognising your limitations.
Jealousy is tamed through generosity.
By practicing mindfulness during the day,
we can begin to recognise the symptoms and apply the antidote.
Setting your intention at the beginning of the day
will help you be attentive to the first sign of these symptoms.

♥

You cannot convince people to love you.
This is an absolute rule.
No one will ever give you love because
you want him or her to give it.
Real love moves freely in both directions.
Don't waste your time on anything else.

Do more of what makes you happy

♥

Happiness is a journey not a destination,
so there is no better time to create your happiest life.
Be inspired to live your happiest life, because when you stop
and look around, this life is pretty amazing.

Happiness is celebrating the little things,
like a handwritten note or beautiful fresh flowers.

The big difference between enjoyment and happiness

♥

Pleasure is always temporary
- and thereby unsatisfying in the long run -
because it's all about immediate fleeting
gratification of the body and ego.

Happiness creates long-haul joy,
because it increases your soul's self-development
- hence the joy lasts as long as you last -
because the joy created becomes an integral part of
who you are as a unique, thriving individual.

Aristotle was a big believer
that every time you behaved immorally
- performing actions your soul is not proud of -
you tarnish your soul.
The worst shape your soul becomes
the worst shape your mood and spirit.
He believed, you cannot be a happy person
if you don't nurture your soul with actions
your soul can be proud of.
Although you might think you can get away with being unkind,
ungenerous, inconsiderate and immoral
- you can never lie to your soul.

Aristotle believed that a person with a good soul
will always more resiliently recover from bad experiences
faster and easier than a badly behaving person of weak character
for the same reason that a physically fit person will more
easily recover from a car accident than an out of shape person.
The person who possesses the virtues of character is
intrinsically emotionally and spiritually stronger.

Aristotle said,
"Thus, it is not enough to perform
one act of generosity in order to be generous;
it is necessary to act constantly
according to the dictates of reason."

♥

Often we make decisions in the moment
without thinking about the long-term consequences.

We humans have conscious insight
which is a powerful protector helping us decide
on how to behave.

Tapping into this unique conscious insight
also means tapping into courage and discipline
so that you can keep growing.

Aristotle said,
"Everyone can become angry - that is easy,
but to be angry with the right person and to the right degree
and at the right time and for the right purpose,
and in the right way
- that is not within everybody's power and not easy."

When Aristotle wrote this, he was admitting
how it's very human to feel negative emotions at times.

It's fine to feel anger, hurt, sadness - as long as you tame
your emotions with rational reason, tamed by human conscious.

If you put an emphasis on money, sex, power, fame, food
- you are making these external values more important
than growing your internal self.
Not only will you not be happy, but your lack of disciplined
character could easily lead to you harming others.
Basically you must learn to live a life
using moderation as your measurement tool
for how much you indulge in a feeling or a habit.

Patience...

♥

Although you may be making internal changes
within your life that might take longer to manifest
- in the same way that planted seeds need time to grow.
During this time of striving for self-change,
it's important you keep reassuring yourself that what you see
with your limited short-term lens is not necessarily
what you are getting in your long-term future.
During this time, it's important to keep yourself focused on the
long-term benefits of your self-growth efforts.

Aristotle said,
"Moreover, this remains true,
no matter how virtuous we become,
for passion is like a wild beast and anger perverts
rulers when they are the best men."

It is important to be self-forgiving
and be focused on persistence not perfection.

Animal magnetism

♥

Since ancient times, animals have been revered as
powerful omens and messengers from the spirit world.
The ancient Egyptians believed cats were their guardians
and protectors, while in early Greece it was thought that dolphins
were messengers from the goddess Aphrodite,
seeking an invitation to love and passion.

Among the Aztecs, the Hopi and the Aymara of Bolivia,
moths and butterflies have signified the presence of souls, of those
who had recently departed or would soon pass from this world.
In many tribal cultures, shamans and sorcerers imitated the
movements of animals in dance and ritual,
adopting the guise of a specific creature in order to awaken
its spirit for assistance with fertility or fortune.

Animals abound in world mythology,
so powerful are their archetypes, and it is thought that
each animal represents a different aspect of human nature.
By learning to observe your fellow creatures
and studying their movements, you can gain wisdom
and instruction on how to live your life.

The animal world had much to teach us.
Some animals are experts at survival and adaptation.
There are times when we can use those same skills.
Some animals never get cancerous conditions.
Some are great nurturers and protectors.
Some have great fertility and others have great gentleness.
Some embody strength and courage,
while others can teach playfulness.

Once you spot the positive quality
in specific animals, you will know what quality
you need to cultivate in yourself.
So the next time you hear a chorus
of frogs start up in the garden,
as well as knowing it may be about to rain,
know that it's also time to cleanse any emotional or
physical baggage from your life.
Or if you see a fox lurking about the back paddock,
realise its sometimes fine to be a little cunning
when the situation demands it.

MIRRORING

♥

♥

"Watch your thoughts, they become words.
Watch your words, they become actions.
Watch your actions, they become habits.
Watch your habits, they become your character.
Watch your character, it becomes your destiny."

AUTHOR UNKOWN

Perception is a mirror, not a fact.
And what you look on is your state of mind, reflected outward.
The world is only in the mind of the maker.
Do not believe it is outside yourself.

Mirroring teaches us that how we
experience relationships and situations in our lives is often
a direct reflection of how we feel internally.
For example, if you believe in yourself, others will believe in you.
If you say hurtful things to yourself, others comments will hurt you,
comments that often have no hurtful intention behind them.
If you respect yourself others will respect you.
Often, when we are upset with others,
it is because we are seeing in them what we don't like
about ourselves. The miracle comes when we stop blaming others
for our unhappiness and are willing to look inward for healing.

To get you closer to your own wholeness,
you must stop pointing the
finger at others and turn inward for guidance.
The negative you see in others reinforces
the darkness you see in yourself.
Through forgiveness you can weaken this darkness.
Once again, strengthen your forgiveness
practice by choosing to perceive love rather than darkness.

Let go of failure...

Think about how often you find yourself
lowering your expectations in an attempt to insulate
yourself against disappointment.
This is typical in our society.
We are often warned against getting
our hopes up for fear of failure.
In these cases the ego is protecting itself by playing
small and hiding from great potential.
The best way out of this ego trick is to reconnect
by reminding yourself that whatever you desire is on its way,
that or something better.
Reconnect with the truth
that the universe is fully supporting you at all times.
Fear of failure is unnecessary.

Trust

Learning to trust in the power that is in you is paramount.
Understand that you are not a separate self
who makes things happen. Instead you are part of an infinite
energy source that everyone can access.
Choosing to access this source of spiritual power
gives you the trust in yourself, not your ego as a guide.
So why attempt to fly with the tiny wings of a sparrow when the
mighty power of an eagle has been given to you.
Have faith in your eagle wings
and allow them to guide your direction.

Honesty

Believe in yourself and have faith
which will keep you away from deceptive thoughts,
and allow you to remain connected to love.
Honesty will keep your perceptions clean
and your actions fueled by love.

Tolerance

The principle of tolerance is all about not judging others.
When an attack thought enters you mind, transform it.
Judgment applies lack of trust and honesty.
Judgment lowers your spiritual connection.

Gentleness

Harm comes from an inner judgment of others
and reflects your own thoughts of yourself.
Harmfulness wipes out the true function of inner peace.
Judgment and harm make you confused, fearful and angry.
Choose against being judgmental
and in turn allow gentleness to pass through you.
The gentleness is an extension of your inner peace.
Who would choose the weakness
that comes from harm in place of the unfailing,
all-encompassing and limitless strength of gentleness.

Joy

Joy is inevitable when you are aligned,
learning to release attack and be gentle.
Gentleness always results in joy.
When an attack thought comes in,
always turn inward for help
and immediately reconnect with joy.

Defenselessness

When your mind grows stronger, your defenses weaken.
No longer defend yourself against the attacks of others.
This is investing in their illusion.
When you think with love, you have nothing to defend against.
When you maintain a defenseless attitude
and choose to see love in your attacker,
it leads you to a state of peace.

Generosity

Generosity is based on trust.
Giving things away is not a loss but a gain.
In the ego's world, the concept of generosity
means to give something up.
In the spiritual world, it means giving away in order to keep.
This is the opposite of what we have been taught by our ego minds.
When we are generous we support our inner peace.

Patience

♥

When you become secure of your inner love,
you no longer fear the future.
This releases your ego's need to fear the future
and hold on to the past.
Forgive the past and accept that love is guiding us forward.
Those who are certain of the outcome can afford to wait,
and wait without anxiety.
Patience is imperative, for it confirms faith.

Faithfulness

♥

All you need is to choose faith in love,
and your readiness will lead the way.
To give up all problems to one answer
is to reverse the thinking of the world entirely.
And that alone is faithfulness.

Open-mindedness

Open-mindedness comes with lack of judgment.
Just as judgment shuts love down, open-mindedness invites love in.
The open-minded can see light where there is darkness
and peace where there is pain.
Through forgiveness the open-minded are set free.

Conquering a mountain of negative thinking

♥

It's no fun going through life ruled by negative
thoughts that in turn create negative experiences.
Climbing out of your negative thought patterns
requires strength and commitment.
With the will to change and the courage to climb,
you can defy the ego's gravitational pull
and reach your higher self.
The goal is to choose to pull your thoughts
to an altitude that is higher than your ego.
Each day your ego is waiting to
attempt to pull you down to its level.

Therefore, embrace the attitude of progress, not perfection,
and if you find yourself falling down a notch or two,
don't fret, just dust yourself off,
lift yourself up and keep on climbing.

A view from the top...

♥

The goal of climbing your way to your higher self
is to permanently change your beliefs.
Prepare for great results
when you start choosing to change your mind.
When your thoughts are aligned with love,
they ignite your good vibrations.
When your vibrations are aligned with great thoughts,
you are 100 per cent attracting great things.
Instead of becoming mired down
in the inevitable challenges of life,
embrace them as opportunities for growth.

CHAPTER
6

EXPECT MIRACLES

♥

♥

"Every time you smile at someone,
it is an action of love,
a gift to that person, a beautiful thing."

MOTHER TERESA

Expect miracles

♥

In life living by your own song strengthens your love...

You know the purity of your own heart and mind.
Now you have to express it. Not through the doings of someone else
but through what you hide. Dare to expose yourself.
What you will see is that the vulnerability that is within you
is within us all. We are all scared to reveal that little us inside.
The one that we only reveal to those who are very close to us.
Look back and see the moments when you let go, when you trusted
and threw your heart with absolute faith at the Universe.
When you felt the hurts and threw your anger to the world,
you released your fears. To open your heart,
cry with pain and surrender to the inner faith of vulnerability.
When you give in. Capture it. Bottle it.
By standing and facing the pain, no matter how hard
and embarrassing it is, you find yourself.

In life you are never alone...

♥

STEP 1

Surrender, stop controlling everything in your life.
This doesn't mean doing nothing,
but it does mean not fretting if nothing is happening.
Accept what is right for your life right now. Let go.
Ask the Universe what it wants to do today,
right now, this minute and trust and act on the answer.

STEP 2

Don't push. Let go of the future.
Listen to your own inner voice and the words and circumstances
around and get on with enjoying your life.

STEP 3

Be happy. Work to follow your joy.
Do what you want, not what you should.

STEP 4

Work on your issues. Forgive yourselves and others.
Set them and yourself free. Write down all your grievances
and resentments and hold the intention to let them go.
Have an emotional fresh start and walk forward in your life.

STEP 5

Love who you are and be who you are.
Know that who you are is good enough.

STEP 6

Be positively grateful. Choose to see the positive in everything.
Only have positive thoughts about yourself and others.

STEP 7

Work on boosting your intuition.

Then love. Get on with your life and don't waste a minute.
If we truly knew everyday the truth
of who we really are we would not hesitate to give love
into everything to the fullest of our capacity.

So choose your direction and set sail.

Loving yourself

♥

Once you start down the road to discovering what loving yourself
really means, life starts to change.
Falling in love with yourself is a journey,
an active adventure that touches every aspect of your life.
Loving yourself completely is the unwavering commitment
to and active expression of:

Knowing yourself

Accepting yourself

Living as the fullest expression of your real me

Self love occurs in the collective power of a series of small things
- actions, beliefs, realisations, and experiences -
and this love will continue
to increase for the rest of your life, if you let it.

Attracting and allowing into your life
only people and situations that support all of the above.

Loving you... what it takes

♥

Be your own best friend. Love hanging out with you.
When you are deeply connected to yourself,
there's no reason to fear being alone.
Do not allow others to take away from you how great you feel,
whether it's family, friends, or a man.

See your magnificence and beauty.
Cherish your own brilliance, without reserve or fear
of it being greater than someone else's light.

Accept your flaws, idiosyncrasies and weaknesses.
Love yourself for who you have been and are.
Forgive yourself for decisions that were not self-supporting.
Acknowledge the dark parts of your life and spirit,
and love them just as they are.

Make decisions guided by self-love.
Take actions only if they uphold your commitment to yourself.
Always be honest about how a relationship
or other situation adds to or distracts from loving yourself.
And if you can't be honest with yourself,
ask a trusted person to advise you,
and actually listen to what that person says.

Change your perspective on beliefs that counter self-love.
Tell those negative voices in your head to go away.
Be willing to believe in the possibility of new possibilities,
ones that breed and nourish love.

♥

*"For unhappy people,
their time is unfilled, open, and uncommitted.
They postpone things and are inefficient,"*

*"For happy people, time is filled and planned.
They are punctual and efficient."*

MICHAEL ARGLE
OXFORD UNIVERSITY PSYCHOLOGIST

♥

Touch

♥

The emotional effect of touch,
being caressed by another person
releases natural opiates in the brain that are
associated with a relaxed frame of mind.
The evolutionary basis for this may lie in our primate past,
around the time of the last common ancestor
of humans and chimpanzees, some five million years ago.
Grooming may well have been as important
for this creature as it is for modern chimpanzees,
which spend hours each day
removing the ticks from each others fur.
This grooming does not merely rid the other chimp of parasites,
it also serves as a reliable sign of friendship.
A preference for such a reliable signal of friendship
would have motivated our furry ancestors to seek out friends.
Those who did not like being groomed
would have found themselves
without allies when it came to a fight.

♥

Venting means talking about unpleasant emotions
in order to make them go away.
People have probably used language
to get things off their chest for thousands of years,
but venting is more than just unburdening yourself
of troublesome thought.
It is the use of language for the explicit purpose
of getting rid of unpleasant emotions.
The idea of venting was pioneered by Sigmund Freud,
who argued that speaking about negative emotions was sometimes
the only way to eliminate them.
Freud's arguments rest on the Hydraulic Theory of Emotion.
Hydraulics is the science of conveying liquids
through pipes and channels,
and the Hydraulic Theory of Emotion views feelings as
mental fluids that circulate around the mind,
much as the blood courses through the veins.
Whenever you hear someone telling you not to bottle
your feelings up, or warning you that you will burst under pressure,
they are implicitly endorsing this view.
As some liquids can easily be converted into vapours,
gaseous metaphors such as letting off steam
can also be pressed into the service of the Hydraulic Theory.

Like it or not we are all animal species.
Darwinian principles apply.
We have evolved into what we are today.
We did not spring ready-made into the twenty-first century.
The human female is born and bred to select a mate,
have babies, and nurture them.
That is why we adorn ourselves, sweep the cave,
attract the best possible male,
fall in love and keep a man at our side as long as we can.
We are hardwired to do it, for the sake of our children.

Whether a woman wants babies or not,
whether she has them or not, is irrelevant.
Her physiology and her emotions behave as if she does.
Her hormones are all set up to make her behave like a
female member of the tribe.
The female brain differs from the male even in appearance.

To fall in love is to succumb to instinct.
Common sense may tell us it's the wrong thing to do.
Still we do it. We can't help it.
Oestrogen levels soar, serotonin plummets.
Ironically, the fall in serotonin is symptomatic of falling in love.
Serotonin, found in chocolate, makes us placid and receptive.
A serotonin drop makes us anxious, eager, and on edge.

CHAPTER
7

CLIMBING
YOUR WAY TO
HIGHER THOUGHTS

♥

105

♥

Everything I lose is found again;
everything that is hurt is healed again.
Everything in my world happened
and it's meant to happen.
Each change or experience teaches me to grow
and leads me to the path I am meant to take ...

♥

Create your own destiny spell

♥

For this spell you will need these ingredients:

A dressing gown or bathrobe
A mirror
Two white candles
A green apple cut in half
A cucumber cut in half
A piece of paper
A pen

The best time to cast this spell is on a Sunday.

Begin by taking a shower,
and then get dressed in your ceremonial gown.
Gather all the items of enchantment
on a flat surface but near the mirror,
so that when you sit down you can see your reflection.
Light the candles.
Pick up the apple and the cucumber,
and breathe in a few deep breaths.
Focus your thoughts on what you would like to achieve in the future.
Think big, and write down your ideas on the piece of paper.

Look into the mirror
and repeat these words:

'I will travel from the depth to the light.
I am my own universe - capable of all things,
I create my own destiny.'

Read out the ideas you have written down,
and add the words:
'I will do this - this is my future.'

Your spell is cast.

♥

I am calm and peaceful inside.
I choose how I feel inside and how I react at all times.
I am worthy of anything I ask for from life.
I believe in me.
I don't let negativity get to me.
Life always gets better when I treat myself better.
I deserve the best in this world
and I treat myself with the respect and love
I willingly give to others.

Affirmations for living my life of love

♥

I care for myself and the world around me.
I love being me.
I forgive and let go.
I am calm and free to be myself.
I bless all that I have, all that I see and all that I meet.
I am wonderful just as I am.
I fill my time doing the things that I love.
I have fun being me.

Taking back control

♥

Know that your life purpose is right inside you.
Think about your life and reflect on who you really are.
If you were to turn your heart inside out
and shake it onto the seat where you are sat,
what would it look like? What would people see?
What would they learn from you?

You can spend decades being someone else,
conforming to the rules of society and its social guidelines.
You will never experience the knowing of absolute happiness
until you became truly the person that you are.
The one that you we born to be.

Every time you blame the world for what you have
or haven't got or what you feel has worked against you,
you are giving away your control,
your power over to others, to circumstances.
If you are out of control
then you will feel like a victim, powerless in your life.
Life will happen to you and you will choose to
beat yourself up again and again and again.
You will hide and blame and get bitter.
If you are out of control you will panic.
So many people have given their power away.
They feel powerless, while life happens all around them
and to them. In their eyes it is not their fault.
Life has just dealt it to them in this way.

What you can do for yourself and others
is to demonstrate that you can be in control.
It doesn't matter what has happened to you, or how bad it has been.
You can take back your power, embrace the universal laws of love.
Remember, experience and learn from your lessons.
Cherish knowing that we are all one,
that you are a magical part of the whole.

Listen to your soul and it will show you the way.
Hold the love in your heart out there in your life for yourself
and the whole world to see. Be brave. Feel the truth in your soul.
Take back control.

CHAPTER 8

MANIFESTING

♥

♥

"Expecting the world to treat you fairly,

because you are a good person

is a little like expecting a bull not to

attack you because you are a vegetarian."

DENNIS WHOLEY
PRODUCER, AUTHOR AND TELEVISION HOST

Mindfullness - taming your mind -

♥

With mindfulness practice, you eventually tame,
calm and befriend your mind, gently taking the reins and steering
it where you want. If you are self-critical and demanding,
you suffer. When the mind gets agitated and negative,
if you are patient and gentle with yourself, it eventually settles down
and you experience something we call peace, and at best happiness.
If you show empathy and kindness your mind calms down.
When you stand back and just watch your thoughts and feelings,
you find yourself less scattered, more anchored and clearer thinking.

Mindfulness means intentionally paying attention,
in the present moment, in a non-judgmental way at yourself.
Rather than running away or repressing negative thoughts and
feelings, you learn to relate to them from a different angle,
experience them through a different lens. By standing back
and being aware, it immediately gives you a new view of your inner
and outer world. By sharpening your focus on what's happening
right now, you start to notice that thoughts are not facts,
they are constantly changing patterns, they come and go,
transform, disperse and dissolve. Thoughts are not who you are,
they are habitual patterns in the mind, nothing more and as soon
as you see them that way, they lose their sting.

Regulating the mind is like driving a car
and constantly having to shift gears
to ever-changing traffic conditions.
Mindfulness teaches you to be aware of what
mental gear you are in and gives you the skills
to disengage and engage when you choose.
The practice of mindfulness
sharpens your focus so you can
do something about your mind being constantly
distracted and mentally hijacked.
You could go through a whole lifetime in your head dreaming
of another life, instead of living your own.

Steve Jobs, the late Chief Executive
of Apple and meditator said,
"Remembering that I'll be dead soon
was the most important tool I ever encountered
to help me make the big choices in life
because almost everything - all external expectations,
all pride, all fear of embarrassment or failure -
all these things just fall away in the face of death,
leaving only what is truly important."

Kindness

♥

Be kind to yourself by intentionally
moving your attention from the mind to the body.
Your body can withstand emotions,
your mind can't because it is hardwired to
come up with a solution when there isn't one.
Think of the body as a safe harbour
when you are being ravaged by negative thoughts.
When you are being possessed
by the demons of your own making,
you should treat yourself like you would treat a friend.
The main thing that calms your mind
is compassion for yourself.

The poet Rumi sums up mindfulness:

THE GUEST HOUSE

This being human is like a guest house.
Every morning a new arrival
A joy, a depression, a meanness,
some momentary awareness comes
as an unexpected visitor.

Welcome and entertain them all!
Even if they're a crowd of sorrows,
who violently sweep your house
empty of its furniture.

Still treat each guest honorably.
He may be cleaning you out
for some new delight.

The dark thought, the shame, the malice.
Meet them at the door laughing,
and invite them in.

Be grateful for whoever comes,
because search has been sent
as a guide from beyond.

Not only is compassion
good for your health,
but the impact of the hormones we produce
in ourselves pass from person to person.
We can pass our neuroses
but we can also pass our feelings
of warmth and kindness.
You get a sudden rush of oxytocin which
makes you feel safe and soothed
and therefore switches it on to
others around you.

Mindfullness

♥

CONNECTION TO FEELINGS

A number of studies have found that
mindfulness results in increased blood flow
to the insula and an increased volume
and density of grey matter.
This is a crucial area that gives the ability
to focus onto your body, and connects you to your feelings,
such as butterflies in your stomach,
or a flutter to the heart.

SELF CONTROL

Researchers have found that
increased blood flow to the anterior cingulate cortex
after just six 30-minute meditation sessions
strengthened connections to this area,
which is crucial for controlling impulse,
helping self control and addictive behavioural patterns.

CONTERACTING HIGH ANXIETY

Researchers from Stanford University
found that after an eight-week mindfulness course
participants had less reactivity in their amygdala
and reported feeling fewer negative emotions.

REGULATING EMOTIONS

The hippocampus is involved
in learning and memory and can help reactivity
to stress leading to more emotional stability.
A researcher from Harvard University coined
the changes to the body that meditation
evokes as the "relaxation response"
basically the opposite to the "stress response."

A story

♥

One evening, a Native American elder
told his grandson about a battle that goes on inside people.
He said, "My son, the battle is between two wolves inside us all.
One is anger, envy, jealousy, sorrow,
regret, greed, arrogance, self-pity, guilt, resentment,
inferiority, lies, false pride, and superiority.
The other is joy, peace, love, hope, serenity, humility, kindness,
benevolence, empathy, generosity, truth and compassion.
The grandson thought about it for a minute
and then asked his grandfather, "which wolf wins?"
The elder simply replied, "the one that you feed."

Born in love

♥

Love is where we all begin.
When we are born, all we know is love.
Our thoughts are lined with love and our minds are peaceful.
Our loving mind believes that all people are equal
and that we are part of something larger than ourselves.
We believe that we are supported and connected to
everything everywhere. We believe that only love is real.
We believe in miracles.

We are born into love
then soon thereafter fear is introduced.
We begin to pick up the fear around us and are led to deny love.
As innocent babies we pick up on fear from the outside world.
With one fearful thought we lose love and are
thereby separated and disassociated from it.
We choose to forget that we are equally as loveable
and worthy as everyone and everything everywhere.

9

KNOWING THE UNIVERSE
HAS YOUR BACK

♥

♥

"Fear less, hope more,

eat less, chew more,

whine less, breathe more,

talk less, love more,

and all good things will be yours."

SWEDISH PROVERB

The worst thing that
thas ever happened to you can be the best thing
that ever happened to you
if you only let it.

Faith is everything.
When you believe in love,
you can relax knowing that it's all good.
Remember that your work is never done.
Each moment offers you an
opportunity to deepen your spiritual connection
and strengthen your mind.

We always have a choice

♥

All of us face challenges in our life.
We do have a choice on how we react to those challenges.
We can look to numerous examples of political
and spiritual leaders who have turned their deep suffering
around to be an inspiration to the world community.
Michelle Bachelet, the president of Chile, survived imprisonment
and torture under the Pinochet regime thirty years ago.
"Because I was a victim of hatred,
I have dedicated my life to reverse that hatred and turn it into
understanding, tolerance and love."

Nelson Mandela spent years in prison for speaking out
against apartheid and racial discrimination. Since being released
from prison he has traveled around the world inspiring people of all
races. He speaks about issues of equality, strength and love.

The Dalai Lama was forced by the Chinese Government
to leave Tibet, his beloved home. The Buddhist people in Tibet
have suffered severe religious persecution, yet the Dalai Lama
teaches love and compassion. He is known throughout the world
for his ability to teach about the power of forgiveness.

Our perception creates our reality and underlines
our choice to be bitter or grateful about what life brings us.
A woman from Cambodia tells a story
where she had to flee political persecution.
She left her family in the middle of the night.
They had to escape so quickly, they could not bring any money
or possessions with them.

They were starving and thirsty after days without food or drink.
They finally came upon soiled rice and contaminated water.
But the woman said they were so grateful
to find food when they were hungry and water to drink
when they were thirsty that they did not see the
food or water as contaminated. There were no feelings
of bitterness about what they had gone through,
only gratitude for how they always found what they needed.
They ate the food and drank the water and did not get sick.

You can choose to work with the power of projection
to raise the spiritual vibration of the world by transforming dense,
dark states of consciousness into lighter,
brighter states of consciousness. We have to set a strong intention
and come from a place of love. We cannot perceive ourselves
as separate from the collective field around us.
To project harmony, we must become harmony.

Serenity

♥

Wouldn't it feel good to wake up without anxiety,
not concerned about what you ate the night before
or if he's going to call you?
Consider the idea of going through the day
without obsessing over the same petty crap.
With a daily commitment to balance, you will be set free.

The first step to rethinking towards balance
is to simply choose balance.
The ego's addictive mind will resist balance at all costs.
You may not realise this, but your number one addiction
might be to thinking. You have more than 60,000 thoughts a day,
and most of them are repeated obsessions
that are totally let loose in your brain. The ego feeds off all those
thoughts and will never let them go until you choose to take a stand.
By giving yourself permission to act out,
you keep yourself stuck in this negative behaviour.
In order to change your behaviour, you must change your mind.
If you are ready to let go of your addictive patterns,
make a fearless commitment to the following affirmation.

I commit to releasing my negative thought patterns.
I choose balance and serenity.

Breathe in -
I commit to relaxing my negative thought patterns.

Breath out -
I choose balance and serenity.

Rethinging your life

♥

To reach a balanced life requires a mental and physical shift.
Your body never truly feels aligned or grounded
when your thoughts are constantly rocking the boat.
When you consciously align your balanced affirmations
with a rebounding exercise,
you will experience a mind-body connection.
This connection will inform your overall
understanding of what it truly feels like to be balanced.
It's in the feeling that the true transformation occurs.

Writing down your thoughts...

♥

Allow your thoughts to flow freely onto a page,
write whatever is in your mind.
Let the writing become a time to release all your chaotic thoughts.
Let your inner guide bring you back to equilibrium
through the flow of each thought that passes through your pen.
The paper can become your trampoline,
where you rebound to a state of mental balance.
Let the words release your mind allowing it to rebound
to a state of balance and serenity.

Time heals wounds but
it is your inner strength that heals your life.

CHAPTER 10

CREATING
YOUR UNIVERSE

♥

"A human being experiences themselves,
their thoughts and feelings,
as something separated from the rest ...
This delusion is a kind of a prison for us ...
Our task must be to free ourselves
from this prison by widening our circles of
compassion to embrace all living creatures
and the whole nature in its beauty."

ALBERT EINSTEIN

Always choose love

♥

The key to maintaining a loving mindset
is to remember that forgiveness is your primary tool.
Whenever you are in doubt,
forgiveness will set you free.
Love is experienced to the extent that we believe in love.
In order to enjoy our own loving experience,
we must commit to keeping our thoughts aligned with love.
Would you rather be right or happy?
When happiness is our primary function,
we turn to forgiveness as the bridge back to peace.
Maintain your loving connection by releasing others.
Each time you feel resentment,
intervene and transform the thought through forgiveness.
By forgiving others you heal yourself.

Remember it is in you...

♥

There is no outside solution to an inside problem.
The biggest gift I have received
is my faith that we are already there.
I hope this book has led you to know
that everything you are seeking is already in you,
and there's no place out there to find it.
Turn inward and ask for guidance.
Undergoing this transformation and restoration
often can feel far out of reach.
Don't get discouraged.
Continue to remind yourself that it isn't far at all.
It's in you right now.
Remain willing to take the necessary steps
to continue turning inward and dealing with the past
to clear all blocks to love.
We take care of the future by living in the present.

With endless love and gratitude,
I send you off with a spiritual connection
of your own understanding -
a connection that will be yours
to grow and share with the world,
an everlasting companion
on your miraculous journey inward.
May you release your fear,
have faith,
and always listen to your inner guide.

Your true colours are beautiful like a rainbow...

♥

"Every end is a new beginning."

PROVERB

♥

Marianne was a luxury and beauty
Public Relations executive in Sydney, Australia.

A career in luxury PR and media gave her the insight
and extrinsic motivation and material for her book writing.
Things We Love is Marianne's fifth book.

Other books include: *Bat Your Eyelashes;*
The Glossy Life; Love. Love Me; and *Talk to Me.*

Her books have sold in the USA, United Kingdom, Europe,
Asia and Australia. Marianne has regularly
appeared as a spokesperson in the media and as a columnist.
Marianne has a postgraduate Masters in
Communications and Psychology. She lives in Sydney.

She would love to hear from you.

Email her on info@batyoureyelashes.com.au
and share your experiences and successes with her today.

Marianne

X